OMOWALI
"The child returns home"

Reconnecting Our Children
With Their True Culture

Martha R. Bireda, Ph.D.
Jaha F. Cummings

blue ocean press
tokyo

Published by:

blue ocean press, an Imprint of Aoishima Research Institute (ARI)
#807-36 Lions Plaza Ebisu
3-25-3 Higashi, Shibuya-ku
Tokyo, Japan 150-0011

mail@aoishima-research.com
URL: http://www.aoishima-research.com

ISBN: 978-4-902837-10-2

Table of Contents

INTRODUCTION

"Separation of a people from their culture breeds illness."
Mary K. Boyd

Our children are in trouble. Of course, not all of them, but enough to consider that African American youth are in a "crisis of values". A crisis in values occurs when youth are alienated from their own cultural values and adopt a value system that does not promote their emotional, social, physical, or spiritual well-being. Many of the problems that our youth experience, regardless of socioeconomic status, have their roots in the inculcation of values that are the antithesis of their true cultural values.

Traditional African American values derive from three sources: our "African-ness", the cultural ethos rooted in our collective unconscious that we

5

have carried and transmitted for generations. These African residuals are so much a part of us that what we often mistakenly believe is a new trend or creation is simply a revival of something deep in our souls. The "American" aspect of our values comes from our experience on American soil; these values, many still with African roots became adapted to the hostile environment in which African Americans had to survive as slaves, then as members of a caste minority. Yet, another aspect of our experience on American soil began to creep in and influence our value system. In our efforts to survive, to thrive, and to be accepted as equals in this new land, we began to identify with and adopt some of the values of the mainstream society. With each aspect of our value system in balance, African Americans maintained cultural integrity and ensured the survival of our culture. All African Americans are attached to the three aspects of our value system in different degrees; in fact, Bell and Evans (1981) describe four distinct interpersonal styles employed by African Americans based upon degree of attachment to traditional cultural values. Their definitions of "acculturated", "bicultural", "traditional", and "culturally immersed" (Afrocentric) are described not as fixed styles but as ways African Americans use to protect themselves in a racially oppressive society.

An individual experiences a crisis in values when the value system is no longer in balance; when his or her identity is shaped more by mainstream values and he or she seeks approval and acceptance through the mechanisms of the mainstream society. An African American is in the midst of a crisis of values when his or her cultural center and worldview of oneness and collectivism is replaced by the mainstream values of individualism and materialism. It is in fact these two values that are reflected in the personalities, the aspirations, and the behavior of far too many African American youth. From wearing overpriced and "branded" clothing to listening to misogynistic rap music, to aspiring to get an education only to "live large" by working for a major corporation, to making money the fast and easy way through drug dealing, African American youth are increasingly identifying success and the "good life" with mainstream values. In their youth and as a result of the lack of proper cultural instruction, they are totally unaware that it is in fact the two values that they are now embracing that were the core motivation for the enslavement and disenfranchisement of their ancestors. Furthermore, these are the values that continue to perpetuate the economic, educational, social, and political disempowerment of African Americans today. Generations of African American youth being attached to the values of individualism and materialism will ultimately lead to the demise of the culture and destruction of the race.

HOW OUR YOUTH LEARN THEIR VALUES

African American youth did not arrive at this juncture of a crisis in values on their own. Somehow over the past 40 years, a disconnect occurred and traditional values ceased to be taught and transmitted to our most recent generations. There are probably many theories about why this occurred, which will not be discussed here. Our focus is on what it is that we can do at this point to reconnect African American youth with what is their true cultural value system, deriving from their African center and their American response to racism and oppression.

I am reminded of an experience I had while working in a low-income community housing project with a group of women, ranging from middle-age to very young women with many children. As the older women laughed and reminisced about the "old days" and all the things that were expected of them, I noticed that that the young women were silent. I asked for their reactions to what they were hearing. Angrily, one responded with a question of "why didn't you all teach us those things?" The women, several mothers of the young women, could only hang their heads as they realized that they had failed their daughters. Yes, we have failed our children by not transmitting to them the beliefs and values that are responsible for our positive strides as a people. Most of us if we are honest will thank one of our parents, family members, or neighbors for calling us to task and ultimately providing us with the wisdom to make the right choices and do the right thing.

Today, African American youth learn their beliefs and values primarily from the mainstream media. They learn what is acceptable, what will make them popular and win approval from the television, and they learn what to believe about themselves and others from rap music. The majority of messages that they receive about who they are to be and what they are to do to be "successful" in life revolve around individualism and materialism. Even the present-day religion glorifies consumerism; worshipers expect material as well as everlasting rewards.

OUR ROLE

The role of adults in the lives of youth are threefold: to provide, protect, and to guide. It is our responsibility to provide for our children's basic needs of food, shelter, clothing, education and healthcare. Our desire to provide has become out of balance however; we now misconstrue giving the unnecessary and often harmful for providing for the basic needs of our children. Overpriced and branded clothing, unreasonably and potentially harmful video games do not fall within the realm of "providing" for our children. Giving our children everything they ask for is not good parenting; good parents are those who can take the heat when they say "no" to their children. It is our responsibility as adults to protect our children from all spiritual, emotional, mental, and physical harm. The purpose of culture is to provide a blueprint for how we are to behave, to resolve problems, to live a fulfilling life. When we fail to pass on to our children the beliefs and values that will protect them, we have failed in our task as a parent. When we allow our children to embrace a set of values that will ultimately harm them, we have failed our children. Finally, our responsibility as adults is to guide our children. That guidance comes through the wisdom that traditional culture provides. The elders for generations have through spiritual connection, intuition, and longevity shared the beliefs and values of the culture so that as a people we could survive and live purposeful, fulfilling lives. When some 40 years ago, as a people with "new civil rights and freedoms, we sought to be accepted as "true Americans", we stopped believing in the value and the power of the "old ways". Our children, at least two generations of them, bear the scars, and more will surely die a "cultural death" if we do not take steps to reconnect them with their true culture.

THE ABANDONMENT OF BLACK CHILDREN

If we do not teach our children our traditional cultural value system, we are abandoning them.

- We do not teach them how to defend themselves. If they were culturally aware they could defend themselves.

- We allow our girls to feel that something is wrong with their features, requiring new features that must be bought and "fixes" endured.

- We allow our boys to feel that their anger against being profiled, targeted, tracked, and disrespected by their teachers and other authority figures is unjustified.

- We allow our sons and daughters to address each other with disrespectful names and we do not stamp this behavior out at its inception.

- We allow our children to disrespect elders (any elders) and do not stamp this behavior out at its inception.

- We allow our children to watch or listen to media in which people disrespect each other, and where our youth disrespect elders and we continue to allow them to watch or listen to it.

- We allow our children to deviate from one of our most important cultural expressions –

greeting and acknowledging the presence of each other. This seemingly small act reinforces our connections to each other as a collective family. By allowing them to believe that they are "individuals" responsible onto and only for themselves, they believe that they do not need to acknowledge each other, and the elders; therefore they believe that they no longer have to maintain "membership" in a "disparaged group" and can enjoy membership in the majority society as long as they are 'individuals'.

- The reality of life in the US, if not in the Americas in general, is that life is still tribal, though the minorities often believe that it is otherwise. The majority culture operates as a tribe, as do the immigrant minorities, but the caste minorities especially African-Americans, Chicanos, and Puerto Ricans often believe that they are members of the majority tribe; and our communities suffer economically, socially, and educationally because of it. In a conglomeration of tribes such as the US, the greater whole ultimately benefits from the cultural, social, economic, and intellectual contributions of the tribes that it is comprised of; but not supporting one's tribe in lieu of dedicating all resources to the majority disempowers one's tribe and ultimately, the greater whole because the full potential of one's tribe is not being contributed to the greater whole. In the US,

19

caste minorities are not stigmatized because they are "American", they are stigmatized because they are caste minorities.

THIS BOOK

This book is intended to be a guide for African American adults; parents, family members, neighbors, teachers; all those who care about our children to help our children reclaim and reconnect with their true identity and true culture. We hope to provide concrete ways that adults can both model and talk to our children about the traditional beliefs and values that will enrich and in many cases save their lives.

In Part I, we focus on "our beliefs", the beliefs of the adult who is reading the book. In Part II we examine the African worldview and why it is important for our children to see the true reality of living in our world. In Part III, we explore twelve core values that adults must model and teach to our children about if they are to reconnect with their true culture. Finally, in Part IV, we talk about the future of our children and our people in the Age of Globalization.

Note: One thing that we must be careful of is viewing the contents of this book as only relevant to those children who are deemed "at-risk", "under-this and that", "impoverished" etc. It is very apparent that we ALL are "at-risk". We are only as strong as our weakest link. Water can seep through any holes in the dike; and these holes lead to the breakage of the entire system. NONE of our children are disposable. It is OUR JOB as ADULTS to be resourceful enough to provide ALL of our children what they need. Any "failed" child is a reflection of the FAILURE of the adults who comprise their social environment.

PART I.

The Transmitters of Culture

*"Our children are who we are,
not who we want them to be."*

Your role as an adult in the community of African people is to provide for, protect, and guide the children who have been sent from the Creator with the knowledge and gifts to carry us forward for generations. Just as for centuries before, the ancestors have passed the beliefs, values, and norms for behavior that have ensured our survival, it is now up to us, the adults, to transmit our culture to our children. It is most disheartening to see and hear our youth describe, and give commentary in the media on what is portrayed in gangsta rap[1] as

---

[1] There is a differentiation between hip-hop and gangsta rap. Those performing hip-hop understand and embrace the responsibility that

"black" culture. Misogyny, violence, drug dealing, hedonism, and general disrespect for ourselves and our elders is not our culture. We are truly in a crisis of values and have abdicated our responsibility to our children and our ancestors when our youth are so confused about their true culture. It is even more sad, when they, our children, are proclaiming to the world what they mistakenly believe to be our culture. When a group possesses "cultural integrity", adults define the culture, and most importantly, children are not mistaken about their cultural identity because the adults who guide them are fully aware of their true culture.

---

comes with delivering the Spoken word, while those performing "gangsta rap" have internalized a foreign value system based on individualistic materialism. Sadly there are some performers who are deemed "hip-hop artists" who actually fall into the category of "gangsta rap" because of their lack of consideration for our community

WHAT IS MY CULTURAL IDENTITY?

We are born into an ethnic group, but we learn a culture. With what culture do I identify? What is my cultural identity? How do I see myself? How attached am I to traditional African American values? How much do I identify with what is African within me? How much do I identify with that in me which is borne out of the suffering of my people in this new land? How much do I identify with the mainstream culture? In order to pass on to my children, the culture of my ancestors, I must first know who I am culturally.

ACCEPTING ADULT RESPONSIBILITY

Just as every person who dies does not become an ancestor because of the nature of their character, every adult is not suited to be a guide for African youth. Guiding our youth is a responsibility that one must believe is his or her duty and willingly accepts. Do I choose to accept the responsibility of being a guide for our children and transmitting our culture? If I do choose to accept this responsibility, then my values must be congruent with those I aspire to teach. If I do not choose to accept the responsibility for guiding African children, then I may embrace any value system that I choose.

CULTURAL BELIEFS AND VALUES

SURVEY

Which of the statements below best reflects your beliefs and values? I believe that……..

<u>A</u>		<u>B</u>
1. My success is the result individual effort only.	Or	My success is the result of my my efforts and those of the many who came before me.
2. My life will be fine in spite the welfare of the majority African Americans.	Or	My life will be impacted by of the welfare of the majority of of African Americans.
3. A successful life is one of purpose, service, and good relationships.	Or	A successful life is one wealth, fame, prestige, and material possessions.
4. My achievements are to to further the cause of African people.	Or	My achievements are for my personal welfare.

27

5. African spirituality connects Or African spirituality is

People to t Creator, all of   superstition and pagan.

6. A person's character is Or   A person's achievements

more important than his   are more important than

or her achievements.   his or her character.

7. Time is money.   Or   Time is the flow and

                                rhythm of life.

8. Looking to the future   Or   Tradition and the past is

preferable to looking   determine our present and

back at the past.   future.

9. Using my head and logic Or   Intuition and hunches are

is the best way to make   important to making

decisions.   decisions.

10. Cooperation and working Or   Competition produces the

together produces the best   best results.

11. Wisdom of the past is most <u>Or</u> Innovation and new ideas
is most important.   are most important.

12. Human beings are one with <u>Or</u> Human beings are separate
nature and all other forms   and distinct from nature and
of life.   all other forms of life.

WHAT DO I BELIEVE?

Take a look at your responses. The following indicate an inclination toward belief in a traditional African American or mainstream value. African American beliefs and values were expressed in: 1B, 2B, 3B, 4 A, 5 A, 6 A, 7B, 8B, 9B, 10A, 11A and 12A. Mainstream beliefs and values were expressed in: 1A, 2A, 3A, 4B, 5B, 6B, 7A, 8A, 9A, 10B, 11B, and 12B.

STATED AND DEMONSTRATED VALUES

It is important to know the difference between who I believe that I am culturally and the cultural person that my behavior indicates that I am. I pass on to my children not the values that I want to cherish as an African American, but the values that they see demonstrated in my attitude and behavior. If we accept the responsibility to truly become cultural guides for our children then we must "walk the talk" or live the cultural values that we aspire to transmit.

OUR CHILDREN ARE WATCHING

- Be the type of woman and man you desire your child to be.

- Take care of your own issues; co-dependency, low self-esteem, etc.

- We cannot give what we do not have. We can only impart love, trust, and acceptance if we feel those things ourselves.

- Remember that our children learn more from what we do than what we say.

PART II.

THE AFRICAN WORLD VIEW

*"Inside all blacks is one heartbeat
that is fueled by the blood of Africa."*
August Wilson

THE AFRICAN WITHIN US

Not so long ago, I attended a service to celebrate the reconstruction and reopening of a Primitive Baptist church that had been destroyed by a hurricane a few years before. As the minister reached his emotional zenith, he waved a red cloth and began a holy dance. I sat mesmerized as I recognized that his movements were the exact same movements that I had seen performed by a dancer in Santiago de Cuba in honor of the Orisha Sango. After 400 years, these two men shared an

African spirit and rhythms deep within the collective cultural consciousness that had been passed by their forebears generation to generation. No matter where we may be in the Diaspora, no matter the national boundaries or the language differences, we are all connected by our African blood.

Intellectually, I have known of the African residuals that influence us all but in that moment, I knew my African-ness not intellectually but at a deep spiritual level. I felt a depth of "knowing" and understanding that I had never experienced before; I knew my "true " self.

While there are many different ethnic groups and languages among Africans, there is a common African worldview. A people's worldview represents the way that group perceives their relationship to the world, nature, and other peoples. The group's worldview provides a way of interpreting reality, relating to others, and a design for living. The worldview is the psychological perspective of a culture and is reflected in the beliefs, values, feelings, and attitudes. The worldview influences how members of the group think, make decisions, behave and define events.

Because civilization began in Africa, this common reality or way of seeing the world commonly known as a "being" orientation, is held by 70% of the peoples who inhabit the earth. The essence of African or being culture is "oneness"; the belief in the connectedness and interdependence of humans and nature. In the African worldview, there is no separation between the spiritual and the material; all things are endowed with the Supreme Life force;

interconnected, and interdependent. The basic human unit is the group and group actions are motivated by and directed toward the collective survival. The essence of life is to be in harmony with one's fellow man, nature, and the universe.

OUR TRUE CULTURAL SELVES

When African Americans are in touch with our true cultural selves, we experience a balance between those values that have their roots in our African souls and those values that were formed as a result of our struggles in this land.

When we are in touch with our true cultural selves, we are not overwhelmed by mainstream values or the desire to be approved and accepted in the mainstream. We are our true to our cultural selves and we do not give up who we are because we know that alienation from our culture will only cause us to be fragmented, marginalized people.

When we are our true selves, African Americans are spiritual, collective, communal, familial, interdependent, and resilient. We are expressive, natural, spontaneous, versatile, flexible, and rhythmic. We are group-oriented, traditional, generous, industrious, resourceful, creative, and persistent. We have respect and reverence for our elders. We believe in the oneness of life and harmony with all things in the Universe. We believe in the power of the seen and the unseen.

When we are alienated from our own culture and have inculcated the values of mainstream, we embrace values that are in direct opposition to our African value system. We embrace individualism, materialism, consumerism, hedonism, and domination. Our view of the world is one of separateness instead of oneness.

It is our duty as adults to become more aware of our African selves; to reclaim and restore our cultural beliefs, values, and norms; and to reconnect with our true selves. In the African

38

worldview, the child is perceived as a "messenger from God". Our children are trying to tell us something; we have strayed from the village too long. It is through our love for and duty to our children that we too will find our way back home.

PART III.

Reconnecting Our Children With Their True Values

"Children are the life-givers, the healers, the messengers of the ancestors. They bring out the spirit of the community - they bring spirit home."
Sobonfu E. Some

When I grew up in the 1950's and 60's, the hope and desire of every African American parent was to give their children a better life than they had experienced growing up. Children have always been considered a blessing in the African American culture. We believe that children are our future.

THE ROLE OF CHILDREN

Children ensure the survival of the group. It is through our children that the group is continued and the culture transmitted. Our very existence as a people is bound to the spiritual, emotional, physical, and cultural well-being of our children. Our children cannot, however, take our people forward if they lack the appropriate cultural knowledge to do so. If our children do not know or practice the culture, how can they ensure its sustainability? We can ill afford as a people to have our children embrace values alien to their true culture and which ultimately threaten our very existence as a people.

To be able to fulfill their purpose and role in the African American community, we must prepare our children by providing them with "primary knowledge", that is the wisdom of the old ways that will assist them in dealing with their present and future lives. There are 12 traditional values that we believe are relevant in our present day and that are essential to transmit to our youth if they are to assume their responsibility to perpetuate the culture. These 12 values are:

- Spirituality
- Family/Kinship
- Community/Collectivism
- Respect for Elders
- Education/Knowledge
- Endurance/Resourcefulness
- Character
- Cultivating Intuition
- Critical Thinking
- Rites of Passage/Initiation

- Purpose

- Power

We will provide suggestions for modeling and directly teaching each of the twelve (12) traditional values. We are writing this book because children play an essential role in African American culture. One of our core values is our "child-centeredness". We will begin by suggesting ways to demonstrate to our children the important role that they play in our families, our communities, and for our future.

HOW DO WE SHOW OUR CHILDREN THAT THEY ARE A GIFT TO OUR FAMILIES AND COMMUNITY?

- **The Most Important Words**

  After "I love you", the most important words that you can say to your child are, "You are special". This does not mean giving the child a false sense of self, pride, or superiority, but rather that you recognize the unique person that he or she is and the very special gifts that they possess.

- **Naming Your Child**

  There is power in the meaning of your child's name. Her or his name can connect them with the ancestors, describe their life purpose, and provide direction for their life.

45

A child's name should be carefully and thoughtfully chosen after seeking guidance from the Creator and the ancestors. Simply putting together a chunk of syllables, adding an accent mark, and

French pronunciation will provide no meaning and direction to a child's life.

In fact, the meaningless of the name could be a poor omen for the child's future.

- *First Teacher*

You are your child's first teacher. It is often said that it is not what we say that a child listens to and learns from, but what we do. If our actions teach a child trust and love, he or she will learn to trust and love. If not she or he will learn distrust and fear. It is important to remember that our child is a very special gift and should be given the very best instruction.

- **Gifts and Talents**

  All human beings are born with a purpose and the gifts and talents to fulfill that purpose. It is your responsibility to observe your child and to seek out those gifts and talents that she will use in the future for the upliftment of the group.

- **High Expectations**

  After "I love you" and "You are special", we must tell our children and mean it, "To whom much is given, much is expected." It is our role to not only observe the gifts of our children but to verbalize our expectations that these gifts will be used in the service of the community.

- *Plant Dreams*

  It is very sad to talk to many teenaged African American youth who have no idea of what gifts or talents they possess and absolutely no dreams for the future. We must begin early to verbalize our dreams for our children.

  For instance, if we recognize artistic interest and/or ability, we might say "I see you as a great artist when you grow up", and of course to the best of our ability provide the tools to help her achieve her dream. Begin early as well to help your child have a broader vision of his or herself than being a sports star or making rap videos. As your child's first teacher you can help shape dreams that are aligned with the culture's expectations.

- **Be There**

  Attend every event that child participates in if at all possible or have a mighty good excuse. The most visible sign of your belief in your child's ability is to "show up".

- *Home Training*

  Provide your children the basic old-fashioned home training that includes not embarrassing themselves, you, your family, or anyone else. Teach them to:

  > Respect themselves.

  > Respect your family.

  > Respect others.

  > Definitely respect the elderly.

- *Hold Fast*

My children are probably the only two adults in their age range who did not see "Eddie Murphy's Raw". It of course didn't hurt them that they didn't see it and they got over the anger. We in fact laugh about their missing that experience. Even if everyone in the neighborhood appears to have gone insane by abdicating their parental authority and responsibility, hold fast to your standards. Monitor movies, television, and music; anything that might bring destructive cultural elements into your home. Remember that you are the parent, not the friend, and that they will get over the anger and love you for caring enough to honor your parental role to protect and guide.

- **Follow Your Instinct**

  African Americans are traditionally intuitive people. We follow our "hunches" and feelings when making decisions. When your intuition tells you not to let your child go our with a certain group or take the car, listen! No matter how disappointed or angry she may get, let your cultural instinct be your guide.

- **Let The Village Help You**

  It was not so long ago that African Americans believed in strict discipline, parental authority, and all adults providing training and discipline for their children. The attachment to cultural values that are less restrictive in childrearing have made a significant difference in the way we now

51

bring up our children. Now days, African American parents become very defensive when an adult attempts to correct their child. Individualism DOES NOT work in bringing up children. You CANNOT raise your children alone. You will need the help of your extended family and the community. Join with other parents of like minds in establishing a core group of parents who agree to parent their children in the village manner.

- ***Teach The 12 Traditional Values***

  Understanding that all children bring the knowledge and the gifts to perpetuate the culture and the group, begin now to model and directly teach the 12 values described in this book.

SOME FINAL THOUGHTS ON MODELING

TRADITIONAL VALUES

I can remember that time when many single women with children took in "roomers". In many cases, these women either had or developed personal relationships with these men. They however, always protected their integrity and that of the family by having these men have separate "rooms" in the house. Probably many of us never really understood those arrangements. Two thoughts:

- ***Respect Your Children***
1. Single women must always remember that if they disrespect themselves and their children as a result of their relationships, they will be disrespected by their children, especially the boys.

2. Single men remember that your sons will treat women the same way in which they see you treat them.

AFRICAN AMERICAN VALUES

The African ethos is spiritual and collective. Children and elders have a special place in the community. The children are gifts to ensure the survival of the group and the elders provide the wisdom that is needed for future generations.

African American values of spirituality, family/kinship networks, children, elders, community, and intuition all have African roots and are considered to be African residuals.

They are all reinforced however in mainstream society due to the oppression that African Americans have endured, the value of education was emphasized as a means of improving the life of African Americans; hard work as a value was reinforced by the belief that African

Americans "have to work twice as hard" to get ahead. Self-reliance and racial solidarity were absolutely necessary in a segregated society. Egalitarian sex roles rather than the more specific African roles were an adaptive value as the result of the economic and socio-political oppression experienced by African Americans. Finally, equality and justice naturally evolved as values for a group of people enslaved and oppressed politically, socially, and economically.

African Americans lost the balance that they had possessed as it related to the integration of the three sources of values during the late 1960's after the Civil Rights Movement promised equality and full citizenship. African Americans began to embrace the mainstream values of individualism, materialism, and consumerism. As African

Americans began to inculcate these values changes could be seen in the treatment of our elderly (less respect), more liberal childrearing practices, individualism in the religious context, less willingness to share with extended families, future orientation (emphasis on upward mobility) and resistance to the idea of responsibility to the group ("I did it, now you pull yourself up by your bootstraps"). The more extensive integration of schools meant that African American children were to be exclusively socialized to espouse a mainstream value system. The most devastating aspect was the totally selfish and actions that resulted from a value system focusing on individualism, materialism, and consumerism: drug dealing in the African American community with no regard to the consequences and the involvement in activities that only benefit the individual that have negative effects on the African American community.

1. SPIRITUALITY

*"Our emphasis [as an African people]
was not on religion, but rather on
spirituality;
and spirituality is higher than religion.*
John Henrik Clarke

Spirituality from the African perspective and from which African Americans derived our value of spirituality is all encompassing. Spirituality is an integral part of everyday life. It has been said that for the "traditional African man, the whole existence is a spiritual one." Spirituality permeates every dimension of African life and the spiritual consciousness is the single most common characteristic of the many diverse groups of African peoples.

In the African worldview, there is no separation between the physical and spiritual world.

In the traditional African view, there exists a hierarchical unity between God, humankind, and nature with God positioned at the head of the hierarchy. Africans have always believed in and worshipped a Supreme Being. Africans were of spiritual systems such as Yoruba, Songhay, and Mandinga before they were Muslims, and Muslims before they were Christians[2].

- **Develop "spirituality".**

  Strive to develop spirituality (connection with the Creator and the spiritual world) as well as religiosity (connection to a religious denomination or church). Spirituality is an

---

[2] With the exception of the Abyssinian (Ethiopian) Church, which preceded the creation of European Christianity in 7 B.C.; it was created in an African worldview and value system.

African American cultural value with traditional African roots.

Talk to elders about "spiritual things".

Introduce your children to the all-encompassing world of African American spirituality.

Attempt to understand rather than judge the spirituality of African peoples.

Begin the study of African and African American spirituality with your children.

ANCESTORS

"If we stand tall it is because we stand on the shoulders of the ancestors."
Yoruba Proverb

Our African cultural beliefs teach us the significance of our ancestors as part of our spiritual life. It is believed that death is an aspect of the cycle of life and that the energy of existence continues beyond the physical life. Our ancestors then are spiritual beings. Ancestor reverence holds an important place in traditional African American culture as it helps us to remember our origins and to ensure our continuity as a people. Reverence for ancestors is an accepted practice for all African-based or "being" cultures. Yet, African Americans give the least amount of credence, attention, and respect to our ancestors. An important aspect of our reconnecting with our true culture and with teaching our children the sacred connection between them and their ancestors will be to begin the observance of ancestral reverence. Ancestors serve as intermediaries between God (Infinite Mystery) and man and can assist us in many ways. They can provide protection, wisdom and guidance as we face life's challenges. Ancestor reverence in no way replaces our worship for the Creator but adds another significant and powerful dimension to our spirituality.

- **Reverence for ancestors:**
  With your children, talk to your elders about your ancestors. Try to

Get the names of as many generations of ancestors as possible.

Ask about their lives and deeds.

Often speak of your ancestors to your children.

Make it a practice to visit the cemetery, take flowers, and pour libations.

- **Ancestral Altar**

Gather the pictures of ancestors, place on a small table.

Place a glass of water on the table and light a candle. Or place flowers on the table as well if there is space.

On birthdays especially, thank your ancestors for your being part of their bloodline.

Thank your ancestors for giving you life and making sacrifices for you.

Ask your ancestors for protection, wisdom, and guidance.

As a family establish a routine of honoring your ancestors.

- **Dreams**

  "Sometimes the ancestors deem certain information so important that they send it to the subconscious mind without being consciously asked."
  Luisah Teish

While dreams are symbolic, they are manifestations of our fears and good dreams are solutions to our problems. Often it is through our dreams that our ancestors come to warn us, or to give us advice. Encourage your children to ask ancestors for advice, to dream and to talk about the meanings of their dreams.

- **Most Important**

Resist the temptation to judge or resist cultural practices that are our own and that are empowering. All over the world, people are reclaiming and reconnecting to their own cultural practices. They have come to understand that the only way a people can truly be conquered or destroyed is through the destruction of its culture. Giving up our African value of spirituality has been disempowering, but it is not too late to reconnect and to have our children understand and reclaim a source of personal power.

2. FAMILY/KINSHIP TIES

"It is family that gives us a deep private sense of belonging. Here we first begin to have our self defined for us.
Howard Thurman

The value of family and kinship ties is deeply rooted in the African cultural ethos. This value survived and was even reinforced in an alien land under the yoke of slavery. It was, in fact, kinship bonds that were a major source of support during the enslavement period. Family relationships of both blood and fictive kin ensure that the physical and emotional support needed by all members is provided. African Americans have a long history of family members sacrificing so that others could attend school or receive support "until they got on their feet." The family is the primary means by which the beliefs, values, and norms of the culture are transmitted; the mother playing a prominent role. Upward mobility, the search for "better neighborhoods" and better jobs has fractured the once common "compound" living arrangements of many African American families. I grew up living in "family compounds" on both sides of my family. I grew up living on a street in a row of houses occupied by myself and my parents, my great-aunt, and my grandparents. When we lived in my father's hometown, we lived on a farm in a valley near my uncle, grandparents, and cousins. This arrangement is now only seen on some of the Sea Islands of South Carolina among the Gullah providing both material and emotional support for all of the family members. While it is probably not possible to return to this form of living today, our children need the familiarity and support of the extended family. If they do not experience the many benefits of the extended family and kinship networks, they will not understand the importance of reclaiming that value. To the best of our ability, despite distance and work schedules, we must try to maintain our extended family ties.

- **Know your kin**

  Make every effort to have your children know "their folks", "kin", and "people". Children need "roots" and "wings". Knowing and interacting with their kin is a means of providing roots.

- **Family trees**

  Construct and discuss family trees. Try to locate long lost kin so that your children will know their people. Make a photograph album to match family members on the family tree.

- **Get together**

  Get together with your extended family often. You don't have to wait until the family reunion. Sunday dinners or family picnics are great ways to stay connected and have your children get to know family members. Do take the children to visit elderly relatives who can no longer travel.

- **Storytime**

  Use family get-togethers as times for children to bond with elders.

Encourage your children to get elders to tell them stories of their lives and stories about ancestors. When possible, make video or audio recordings of the storytelling. This will be an invaluable oral history that can be passed generation to generation.

- **Family Books**

  Have the children in the family interview elders and write family books. Keep records of all the accomplishments of family members. This becomes part of the written history of the family. Don't forget to keep the family Bible current.

- **Naming**

  The highest honor you can pay an elder or an ancestor is to name your child after them. I have a first name that has been passed down for four generations and the older I become, the more of an honor it is to have been named for both of my great-grandmothers and grandmother. Choose an elder or ancestor that has the qualities that you would like your child to have and name the child in that person's honor.

- **Collective prosperity**

  I have an elder cousin whose family of eight children are all very successful in their own right and as a family.

From early on, they have joined each other in business ventures and have come to operate as a "family cooperative". I once asked her the secret to her children working so well together. She replied, "I told them when they were children, if one is a millionaire, all of you are millionaires." They understood the African value of collectivism; that their gifts, talents, and hard work was to benefit the collective rather than only themselves as individuals.

- **Family Talents**

  As each generation educates their children, we often forget the special talents possessed by our ancestors that supported the family and made it possible for each generation to have a better life.

Have the elders talk to your children and when possible teach them some of the talents of which the ancestors were proud. Don't let the last aunt pass on before teaching the children in the family how to make quilts or the uncle before teaching the children how to do wood carvings.

THE FAMILY UNIT

- **Working together**

Families of ten or three only work efficiently if all of the members contribute. Part of giving children chores to do is to teach the values of cooperation, reciprocity, and group responsibility. I once had to let my children learn the importance of working together through "logical consequences". Each evening I would beg them to go ahead and wash the dishes and take out the trash. They would play around until it was time for bath and bed and the kitchen would remain unclean. Finally I had enough and announced that we would work together as a family or it would be "every man for himself". Well, they left the kitchen undone once more; I announced the next day that since they preferred for every man to be for himself that I would shop only for me, cook and do laundry only for myself. It only took that one time for them to understand the value of cooperation.

- **Eat meals together.**

My son was in the 11th grade before he discovered from some of his classmates that all families did not sit down to eat meals together. He was thoroughly shocked because he assumed that this was what all families did. Sitting and eating together while discussing your children's day or current events is one of the most important things that families can do. Unless it absolutely cannot be avoided, eat meals together. Working extra jobs that take parents away from mealtimes together simply to buy more things demonstrates the value of materialism. The time spent with your children, not the amount of things bought for them teaches the value of family. They will only be able to pass on what they know.

- **Family rituals**

Find some small thing that is special to you as a family and make it a practice. It can be as simple as a special way of greeting each other or each child having "his" or "her" day. When my children were young, we had a special way of coming together and hugging each other called "caterpillar". When one of us needed a hug, we called "caterpillar" and it felt wonderful.

- **Time vs. things**

When I talk to my children, both adults now, about their childhood, they always remember the trips taken together or the special times spent together. They never mention something that was bought for them! I had a philosophy that toys would break and fancy clothes would be outgrown, but experiences would last forever. I know that to be the case.

3. COLLECTIVISM/COMMUNITY

" I am because we are."

African Proverb

The core value derived from our African roots is oneness; our connection to all things, God, our ancestors, man, and nature. The one value that most demonstrates the African worldview and the African American culture is collectivism. Collectivism describes the African American American is collectivism. Collectivism describes the African American sense of "community". The collectivist cultural orientation emphasizes the group as the most important social unit and decisions are made for the good of the group. Our cultural value of collectivism or community is demonstrated by the "we" consciousness of African

Americans, our identity with the group, and the expectation that we are to care for those less fortunate than ourselves, that we do not forget from whence we came, and that we "give back" to our people.

It has been said that the inner self of the African is longing for community. We look for a sense of belonging and we seek affiliation with others in the group. Our group needed to feel loved, needed, valued, and respected; all of which occurred in the "villages" in which many of us grew up. Today our children go to schools where they do not feel accepted or connected; they spend hours in solitary play with video games on the computer or watching television instead of playing outdoors with groups of children. It is because of the loss of community and the sense of belonging to a group that our youth form their own communities which we call "gangs" and seek the sense of security that many of us experienced by being part of a cohesive community.

INDIVIDUALISM

The antithesis of the African American value of collectivism is individualism. African-ness is essentially, "connected-ness". Our cultural institutional and personal relationships are based on our "connections to". This is the glue that holds us together. Individualism is "separate-ness from". This neutralizes the glue that holds us together. The necessity of our children unlearning the individualism of mainstream culture is of paramount importance to our solvency as a people. We have not taken this seriously enough up until now. We have been saying the mantra "the more we are like them, the better off we will be"; and we are tangibly, as a people, in the worst cultural, social, spiritual, economic, and ecological shape that we have ever been in. Even in slave society, we recreated families through the adoption of each other as brothers and sisters; but now "we" has become "I", and our children are suffering the pain of being "connected" stock alone in the world as "disconnected" people.

ANXIETY

Possessiveness and Materialism result from the separation of a people and their connections. The individual only has influence over the self. As a means of satisfying power needs, and in order to accommodate expansion of self outside the boundaries of self without, Possession becomes the objective. The more the individual owns, the more the individual believes he has control over life. In becoming an individual, however, the individual gives up the freedom to actualize true self.[3]

[3] From Cummings, J.F. (2008) How to Rule the World: Lessons in Conquest for the Modern Prince. Tokyo: blue ocean press.

DETACHMENT FROM NATURE AND ANXIETY

Eliminating our children's connection to the natural environment contributes to a sense of detachment from others. The presence of nature in one's environment is a constant reminder of the delicate balance that must be maintained between people and the natural environment that sustains them. Living in concrete jungles devoid of green only adds to feelings of loneliness and separation, moreover, the anxiety of an oppositional relationship between other (as promoted in an individualistic culture). If children cannot see Nature, they will be more likely to lack hope. In this scenario, life can be seen as a confrontational, competitive race to expand and acquire more and more, as an attempt to reach inner peace. Those who cannot readily access the Hope-giving peace of Nature can be in a constant state of anxiety and stress; and there can be a higher likelihood of mental problems developing, either as a reaction to, or as a means of dealing with the constant state of external agitation. In this scenario, one can become very externally-oriented and can attempt to reconcile this state of agitation through "winning" and having an edge over the competition (everybody else), which will come from the possessing and consumption of material icons, or through relationships in which they can dominate others.[4]

4 Ibid.

BUSINESS AND COMMUNITY

We must teach our children the importance of collective economics. Like mentioned earlier, the world is made of "tribes". Tribes are groups of people, communities, who collectively endeavor towards the sustainability of their group. Our children must understand that there is no success without collective success. Like in nature, a monocrop is susceptible to all the same dangers, while a diverse variety of crops has a much greater survivability. If we teach them to operate collectively, collective strengths and weaknesses will bring balance so that economic viability will always be a reality. We must teach them that business is one of the aspects of our community, hence is responsible to the sustainability of the community and the community is responsible to the sustainability of the business. This is collective economics.

Even though businesses are "privately-owned", they are still community-owned, because people grow to depend on them to meet their needs, hence creating a social economy. Because businesses are made up of people, they are "living" institutions bound to the same responsibilities and obligations as others in the society.

Our children must also be taught all businesses that operate in our community must respect our collective business culture, otherwise the whole community is at risk. In not doing so, these businesses, from our perspective, embody the Culture of Individualism; and cannot be expected to act accordingly, because there is nothing to compel them to act in a manner that is respectful of the viability of our community, culture, and environment. When the Culture of Individualism is promoted, businesspersons in the community will lose the feeling of community responsibility inherent to those communities and societies that are collectivist. Businesses that are freed of these connections become focused solely on profit. Once business owners realize the monetary gains that come with not acknowledging their responsibility in the social economy they can readily be persuaded to separate themselves further and operate "freely" and in "free enterprises". Without the concurrent application of codified law to a local business culture that has exchanged its collectivist value system for that of individualism, any actions that businesses take, such as disrupting the balance of society and mismanaging the environment, would not be considered transgressions against society unless they are judged to break codified law. Even if they are aware of codified legal environment that they have to maneuver in, with the internalization of an individualistic values system, they are "freed" of any responsibility to the community that they would have formerly been liable to as a "member of the community".

Collectivism/Community is a value that must be taught with consistency over the child's life. In the adolescent years, peer pressure can have a negative influence on a child's behavior and worldview (unless the parents collectively disallow a large number of children from embodying anti-cultural behaviors), therefore some children may appear to stray from this value, but if it is embedded in their psyche and the community does not allow them to go too far outside of themselves without censure, they will come back; because as young adults they will want to enjoy the security that the collective provides in allowing them a safer space from which they can put forth effort to actualize their dreams.

WHAT CHILDREN FROM COLLECTIVE CULTURES MUST BE TAUGHT

1. My identity comes from my connection to my group.

2. I have an obligation to "give back" to my community.

3. I am endowed with gifts and talents to be used in service to my community.

4. I should never do anything to benefit myself that will harm others in my family or community.

5. I am always connected to my brothers and sisters no matter how much status and wealth I attain.

6. I have an obligation to help those less fortunate than myself.

HOW DO WE TEACH THE VALUE OF COMMUNITY?

- *Teach Empathy*

  When your child judges or mistreats others, ask "how would you feel?' Talk about how our actions can hurt others. Do not yourself or allow your children to speak ill of those less fortunate than you. If your children have great privilege, take them to see and experience the lives of others less fortunate. Emphasize: "But by the will of God, go I".

- **Be an example**

    Practice the art of "community". Give to the homeless, volunteer at homeless shelters. At the end of every season, give clothing and toys to those less fortunate. Let your children see you give to charities and needy people. Involve them in the process.

- **Giving Back**

    Talk to your child about his or her obligation to give back to the community. Be the best teacher of this value yourself. Find a project that you and your children can work on in the community.

- *Teach our history*

  Buy books about and discuss the lives of those who unselfishly sacrificed for the good of the community. Every African child should be aware of the struggles of African people and especially the Civil Rights Movement

- *Logical consequences*

  Teach children through "logical consequences" what happens when we are selfish and do not share with others. Make sure your child knows that it is because of selfishness and individualism that our communities face problems such as drug dealing, theft, etc.

- *Group solidarity*

  Don't just talk about it, buy Black; support the African professionals and merchants in your community. Your children will see this value in action.

- *Teach trust for group members*

  Show your children through your example that Africans can work together. Establish or join a revolving loan club. Help the youth in your community establish such a club to start teaching early the importance of trust and working together for the benefit of all.

- *Harmony with nature*

Take your children out to nature. Let them play in greens, browns, reds, yellows, blues, and blacks of the natural environment. Let them feel the connections to the earth, to the ocean, the sky. Take them to see animals on farm, and to fields filled with crops, and to the fishing docks. Show them where their food comes from. Take them to a waste treatment plants or municipal dump. Let them see where waste goes. Take them to a forest and to river and show where their water comes from. Take them to a desert; show them what the earth looks like with little water. Teach them that when they need solace, when they need positive energy, and place to be quiet, that they can go to the ocean, to the park, to the lake, to the desert, to the river, to the mountains, and be at peace. Teach them the importance of their connections to the earth and its importance to our lives.

4. RESPECT FOR ELDERS

"Our connection with our elders is a deep and ancient one. We honor our elders most when we use their gifts to build a life filled with integrity and accomplishment."
Robert Fleming

ELDERS

The importance of Elders must be reestablished in all of our social relations. This process can be initiated through the renaming of ourselves. Adult women are to addressed as "Mama" or "Iya"; and adult men are to be addressed as "Baba", regardless of blood relationship. This renaming is not only for children, but also for the adults. If our men and women address each other as Mother and Father, the entire social dynamic changes. As mentioned in the section on Naming:

when a child hears their name, they are reminded of their destiny. When we hear our name as "Mama" or "Baba", we are reminded of our social role. We are every child's parents, and we are each other's partners in raising the children. A man who addresses a woman as "Mama" or "Iya" cannot disrespect her by virtue her social role; and a women who addresses a man as "Baba" cannot disrespect him by virtue of his social role.

Upon reaching "elderhood", additional deference is granted. Elders are the possessors of our collective experience and can translate these experiences into life lessons that can be shared with those younger than themselves. Elders share their profound wisdom accumulated throughout their life experiences with the community, and teach children essential lessons through the sharing of

104

stories of these experiences and those of other elders and ancestors.

In the same way that renaming sets up a self-checking social dynamic in which the speaker of the name and the owner of name are bound together in a social roles created by those names, the ritual of asking permission to speak in front of a group from elders creates a similar dynamic. When asking an elder present permission to speak in front of the group, the requester is then humbled so that they will be mindful of the words that they use in front of the audience. This is not to censure the requester, but instead to push him or her to aspire to higher levels of communicative prowess and to ensure that the content of the message being shared is of the highest caliber.

Also, when speaking in front of groups of people not of our culture and an elder is present, one will 1) not speak in a way as to embarrass the elder and 2) not allow others to speak to them in the way that either would cause an elder to be subjected to comments that will cause them pain, or if so, satisfactorily address these issues so that they can feel that the younger generations are making progress from their past efforts.

Elders are the vision and the wisdom keepers. In African culture, the family structure is hierarchical based upon age and authority; one's status increases with age. Elders have the highest authority; they are closest to the ancestors. As ancestors, they can intercede and assist us in our lives. We should give them the respect that they deserve in preparation for their new roles.

SUGGESTIONS FOR TEACHING RESPECT OF THE ELDERLY

- Take children on visits to elderly relatives.

- Take children on visits to nursing homes to talk to elders. In our culture all Elders are our grandmothers and grandfathers.

- Take children to help the elderly with shopping and cleaning on weekends.

- From time to time have children prepare meals for some of the elderly in their neighborhood.

- Have children spend time with a variety of elders so that they can learn form a variety of life experiences, and so that the elders may enjoy imparting knowledge to the upcoming generation.

5. EDUCATION & KNOWLEDGE

"The function of education is to teach one to think intensively and to think critically. Intelligence plus character – that is the true goal of education."

Martin Luther King Jr.

In African cultures, the most important component of child's intellectual and spiritual life is in the discovery of his or her passion, or dreams. It is from knowledge of this that the adults in the community design the child's educational offerings to fit the cultivation of this young mind and offer support, advice, and encouragement in this field of study so that he or she con contribute their creative gifts to the community and enrich the lives of all.

In the current setting we have turned our children over to people who only desire to turn our children into present and future consumers. From their perspective, a successful education is gauged by the effective 1) socialization of the child into being an "alone" individual whose purpose is to get a "job" and consume and/or be a long-term client of the corrections system and produce products as a vassal of the state via privatized prison systems; and 2) "performance"-based education measured through standardized testing which only develops competency in performing on these tests at the expense of cultivating critical thinking, life-long learning skills, and creative arts such as art, music, dance, and physical education. Our children are being turned into automatons free of our cultural value system. They internalize the individualistic and materialistic values and the interests of the majority culture. They are ready for life in job that does not utilize their innate creativity; or enlist military service as an escape, it often being an employer of those youth either devoid of imagination, hope, or other choices; rather than as a proactive decision to serve in the military as a career choice; or as a prisoner.

Reaching one's potential through educational achievement has been a core value of African Americans. Rooted in the "formal" African educational tradition of such universities as the University of Sankore (Timbuktu), etc. and in the "informal" educational tradition of multi-year professional apprenticeships, African Americans believed that a good education was the key to a better life. Most importantly, the traditional African

American belief about education was that while times and situations may change, your education was the one thing that could not be taken from you. Equally important, education was viewed as a "revolutionary" activity. Becoming literate and educated means more than a means to a job, it provides mental freedom and promotes critical thinking. A truly literate man is always a free man.

KNOWLEDGE

- Our children must be taught how to reason, how to critically think.

- They must be taught the importance of life-long learning.

- They must be taught about the importance and joy that comes from the constant honing of one's craft – skills, gifts & talents.

OUR WORLDVIEW

If the school does not teach the philosophy of our people, who will?

- To be an educated person of African descent, our children must be familiar with our philosophies and worldviews.

- Our children must be made familiar with the history and philosophy of ancestors of the ancient world and of recent history.

- Our children must be made familiar with the history and philosophy of our ancestors and our ancestors of the Diaspora.

- They must be made familiar with political, cultural, economic, scientific, spiritual, and resistance movements of both the Continent and of the Diaspora.

- They must be made familiar with our philosophers and political leaders, and have them contemplate the world from the perspective of these thinkers and then devise their own views on the world.

- Our children must know that there is no "universal" way to think. This is the power of the mainstream culture over our children. They are taught to believe that what they are being taught is school comes from an "objective" perspective; free of culture; free of political, economic, and social interests; and free of social power dynamics. They must know that they exist in this world, and are not pathological variations of the "universal" model for humanity that they are taught, they are not, in the schools and in the society as a whole.

- Our children must know that life is an exercise in high self-esteem. They must know that how one perceives them self impacts greatly on them greatly - what decisions one makes and how people treat them. Self-assured, critical-minded, and politically astute people are still subject to the ways of the world, but are less likely to be victimized more than one time...

- Through education, we can teach children to cultivate their knowledge in the academic, vocational, and cultural subjects that relate to their dreams, and with this knowledge and determination, they can actualize their creative potential.

EDUCATION AND POWER

On this note, a few years ago the authors went to the island-nation of Kanaky, the French Overseas Territory of Nouvelle Caledonie (New Caledonia), which incidentally is part of the African Diaspora in the Pacific. We met with the Minister of Culture of the Provisional (Indigenous) Government. We asked her if there were any juvenile detention centers or institutions of that sort for Kanak youth. She looked at us first like we were crazy, then had a big laugh. She then said that "we cannot lose even one of our children". She then proceeded to share with us that they had to reclaim their youth from the French and bring them back to the villages where they are educated until they are eighteen years old. Then they go to university in the capital, Noumea. They do this because they realize the crisis of values that their children were experiencing, being taught materialism and individualism in the state schools, being of a collective culture. To protect their children they recognized this, took back control of educating and socializing their children. They also added an additional component to their education, a thorough understanding of power and one's responsibility to one's family, community, and cultural nation. This additional component was the implementation of the training of EVERY CHILD in the chief's education. This education is the set of skills required of a future chief in order to lead their people and ensure that all of the needs of the people are met. Because they are in a French colonial paradigm, it is not certain where whom will be placed or be in their life, so all children are empowered with the knowledge, wisdom, and personal power to be a leader, and take ownership of it. The Kanak are part of our African family, and endure a similar "battle of ideas" that we are enduring, and give us a positive example of a community's decision to cultivate EVERY child, leave none behind, and take ownership of the worldview and value system that their children are learning.

MODEL THE VALUE OF EDUCATION BY:

1. Reading... yourself...

2. Having a Black library in your home.

3. Setting time aside for family reading and discussion.

TEACH THE VALUE OF EDUCATION BY:

1. No if's, and's, or but's, your child's JOB is going to school and performing well (producing). Like you go to work to produce and contribute to the family, your child's responsibility is to go to school to learn the skills necessary to contribute to the family and the community in the future.

2. The hours between coming home from school and bedtime are to prioritized as:

    Homework

    Reading For enjoyment

    Chores

    Family Dinner/discussion

    Bath and preparing clothes for next day

3. During the week there is no time for ANY television, video games or surfing the net.

4. Debunk the "acting white myth". As Africans, our educational lineage precedes that of Europe by thousands of years. Both ancient and modern Europe (ancient Greece and Moorish Spain) depended on the intellectual offerings of African universities to construct the curricula of their own education systems. Do not allow your child for one minute to believe that by studying, they are "acting white". By doing so, you would be doing a grand disservice to both your child and to our ancestors.

5. Allow your child to associate only with the children of a core group of parents who will ensure the following of the same rules, etc.

6. ENDURANCE/ RESOURCEFULNESS

"Now faith is the substance of things hoped for, the evidence of things not seen. For by it the elders obtained a good testimony"
Hebrews 11:1-2

Through a long history of struggle in this country, African Americans have developed the ability to withstand hardship and adversity. Sorrow, pain, and hardship are considered a part of life and cannot be avoided. Africans in this land have for generations been taught to face disappointment, tragedy, and defeat with dignity and resolve. Just as the ancestors have taught us to "keep on keeping on", we must teach the children to persist, to be creative, and to resourceful until they overcome. In this age of instant everything and the attitude of entitlement, teaching the value of endurance can be difficult, however, with love and guidance it can be done.

FAITH

We would not be here if not for the faith of our ancestors. The elders understand that it is the spiritual quality of faith that has helped us persist and overcome in the struggle that our people have faced. Talk to your child about the struggles of African people and emphasize the role that our faith has played. When they are faced with any difficulty, talk to him about the importance of being that "this too shall pass". Talk to her about how your faith has helped you to overcome in the past.

PATIENCE

A significant aspect of faith is patience. In this "instant" society, where we assume that everything that we will desire will come quickly, our children have lost the ability to have patience. If they do not have patience they cannot practice the attribute of faith and they will not develop the value of endurance. Use your judgment in making them wait; for anything that which is not absolutely necessary for their survival and well-being, they can wait. Do not be afraid to be the adult guide and teach the lessons that it is your responsibility to teach.

RESOURCEFULNESS

One of the things that is beautiful and loved and respected about African Americans is their ability to "turn dust into gold". Out of necessity, during slavery we had to cultivate our innate abilities to create something out of nothing in order to survive. In less trying circumstances, this same trait has led to the development of artistic and fashion trends that have been the envy of the world. Sadly we have not passed this trait down to our children. Instead of priding oneself on their ability to call forth this ability and *create* their own style and way of life, today's youth only *consume*. They crave ready-made branded products and desire to watch and listen to cut-and-paste music and art.

What made Black people beautiful in the past was the ability to *innovate*. Now we are seen in mass media as the ambassadors of consumption and materialism. This is a violation of our inner essence. We as Africans have the spiritual ability to call forth intuition and co-create, we instead have traded this ability for the lazy approach, consuming ready-made identities.

Young men used to pride themselves on their own individual fashion, now they wear other men's names on their backs and wear "play" clothes as formal wear. Our young women now buy hair colors and textures that are incongruent with their features, and buy brand name clothes and accessories that do not coordinate well with their beautiful skin tones and features.

We used to not have to "consume" so much, but now we need to constantly buy bigger and newer things, because that space that used to be filled with our creative aspirations is now a void growing ever bigger through the externalization of our identities.

Our people used to be able to fabricate anything, and create beauty from ugliness. Our cousins in Cuba are able to still drive cars from the 1950s. They are able to fabricate new parts and keep them running smoothly, despite by the fifty year US blockade.

Our children cannot even dance well anymore. Our level of artistic production has become so marginal that anyone can appropriate and take ownership of our cultural productions; our music, art, and dance. Not only do we turn it over to the majority culture's economy, but we have given away the sanction of usership that we used to possess.

We are not a marginal people. Even in our present, ill-effected state, our cultural forms can be found around the world from our natural hair styles, to our dress, our dance, our lyrical and oratorical styles. But unless we do something soon, we will no longer be needed, because our level of cultural production will be so marginal that it is no longer "special" and reflective of our African-ness.

What makes the world beautiful is its diversity. If we surrender this to a Culture of Nothing, a culture of consumption versus creation, a culture of materialism versus collectivity, there will be no consumer use for us, and the human family will lose an essential part of its intellectual and creative capacity.

Though the promoters of the Culture of Nothing may profess that it is in the best interest of humanity to become the same, speak the same, eat the same, dress the same, own the same, die the same, an indisputable fact of nature is that diversity is necessary for life, and monocultures die away. Though a monoculture may protect a particular strength, it, as a whole, also has the same weakness. Hence, when adversity, i.e. disease, adverse weather conditions, scarcity of a needed item comes, the whole group dies out. This is what happened with the Irish Potato Famine and all the other experiments to create one identity. In the case of the Irish Potato Famine, the Potato Blight struck, and since all of the potatoes had the same genetic structure, they all died. In the human family, this translates into the reality that each human cultural group has something to contribute to the human family. If it is not cultivated or able to share its particular knowledges the human family lacks this, and the result is that all share in the same weakness.

We and the world-at-large cannot afford for us to become clones of the majority culture. Though they may desire it, it is not in either our or their interests.

Not having control of institutional power has required that we achieve greatness and not accept marginality, where those who do, have to option to being marginal because the apparatus of control will still work for them. Where in our case now, though our children do not have institutional power working for them, they have been taught to believe that they share in its interest and benefits and it has allowed them to lower the expectations for themselves. And because we have turned them over to educators who expect them not to achieve and because many of us believe this as well, our children do not rise to the occasion like they should.

Children have to ultimate capacity for creativity, because their imagination has not been stifled. If we allow our children's imagination to be destroyed and give them video screens to replace their own thoughts, dreams, and imagination with images to consume, we are committing a crime against humanity. We are killing our children's ability to actualize themselves as whole people. We make them dependent on direction from projected images that are designed to deny more and more of their creativity and replace it with an insatiable desire to consume and imitate.

In doing so, we are destroying one of our most important and beautiful cultural traits, our resourcefulness.

HOW TO TEACH ABOUT ENDURANCE AND RESOURCEFULNESS:

- **Delayed gratification**

  Help your child learn endurance by requiring him to earn or to wait for something special that he desires. This process teaches patience, teaches that disappointment is part of reality, and can assist in teaching a child the difference between wants and needs.

- **Needs and Wants**

  It is your obligation as a parent to provide for your child's needs. In this age of consumerism, we often confuse wants with needs. In our desire to give our children a better life than we had, we have lost balance. We are creating generations of children who expect to get everything that they want. We as adults surely must know that nobody gets everything in the way he or she wants it. Start early to help your child understand one of life's realities.

- **_Keep Trying_**

  Every now and then, give your child a task to do that is just a little above her ability. Encourage her, don't let her quit, and watch the smile of pride when she succeeds.

- **_Encourage Creativity_**

  Are you preparing your child to live in a changing world? How will they cope if a natural disaster occurs, or if your financial situation changes drastically? Probably most important, can your child make his own toy or write her own little picture book? If your child's only creativity comes from playing video games and surfing the net, then he will surely not develop the resourcefulness or even the attention span needed to persist in times of hardship.

7. CHARACTER

"Good character alone separates humans from the lower animals. Apart from good character persons do not exist."
Idowu

Character is moral or ethical strength; integrity. The values that a child learns are very important because the type of values that he or she possesses will determine the strength of his or her character. Attachment to our traditional African-centered cultural values can produce a person of good character. The character of an African American should always produce actions that are beneficial to our community.

CHARACTER IN THE IFA TRADITION

These 16 principles of character of paths to enlightenment come from the ancient Ifa Tradition of the Yoruba people of Nigeria. Knowledge, contemplation, and internalization of the verses can bring about "deepness and change". Use these 16 principles as a way to reflect upon your character and bring about personal change. After which, you should teach these to your children. These principles will be there guides in the work to maintain *Iwa Pele*, good character, throughout their lives.

1. Whatever degree of material possessions in life, without good character, it is all meaningless, worthless.

2. Behave gently and with consideration so that you may live and rest quietly in your home.

3. Strive continually to attain the absolute truth even while experiencing the tribulations of life.

4. No matter what, we must be skillful. By being skillful we minimize the obstacles in life and maximize our happiness.

5. Be alert to your shortcomings and weaknesses. Face the real source of your problems.

6. One's character is that which determines his or her fortune in the world. For the improvement of Life, one most improve his or her character; one must improve his or her behavior.

7. Do not practice deception or be in the habit of telling lies; be frank and honest in situations.

8. Stubbornness is not beneficial; listen to the truth about yourself. Do not disregard well-intended advice.

9. Anger does not do anything for anyone; patience is the parent of good character.

10. Strive continually to achieve the impossible; struggle endlessly to improve your destiny.

11. Guard well against dishonorable acts that may ruin your reputation.

12. Learn to act more and react less: reacting based on the ways of others leads to misfortune.

13. The ancients state that it is time we actually live the truth and not merely believe it.

14. Strive to develop gentle and balanced character in order to win the rope of life.

15. Endeavor earnestly to exercise diplomacy in all matters and at all times.

16. Ifa states that we must not meet force with force nor practice bad medicine. We are to sit quietly and exercise spirit.

If your child is taught the 16 principles of character according to the Ifa tradition, then he or she will become an adult of good character and a treasure to their community.

8. CULTIVATING INTUITION

"The really valuable method of thought to arrive at a logically coherent system is intuition."
Albert Einstein

CULTIVATING INTUITION

As African people we have a natural propensity towards intuitive conversation with each other, and intuition as a fully developed part of our intellectual capacity. We and especially our children have been dumbed down by the disproportionate emphasis on left-brain skill development while neglecting our right-brain skill development. An essential component of African intellectual development is the alignment of "head" and "heart", i.e. left (analytical) and right (intuitive) brains. Any deficiency of either one leads to an inability to "think". Thinking is the ability to align the two aspects of perception and analysis and call forth thought and action.

Our children are told that their feelings are invalid and that they are somehow supposed to make sense of a pathological social and educational environment. By doing so, we negate our children's ability to recognize Truth, and to call upon extrasensory perceptive abilities that are easily accessed by African people, if cultivated.

We must teach our children the difference between thoughts, feelings, and emotions and their role in life. Feelings are messengers that inform us of the congruence or incongruence of an object, person, or situation to our Personal Truths. We are to thank them for informing us of a particular dynamic and then return. Emotions are the passionate energy that we call upon to assist in proactive tasks. Feelings and Emotions are only problematic when we forget that we are the center of our lives and they are messengers, and cede our personal power to them. Being more proactive than reactionary is what brings the relationships between our Higher Selves and our Feelings and Emotions into balance.

It is very important to reiterate that all of our children's feelings are valid; because they are children, they must just be taught how to balance the information that feelings provide with thoughtful contemplative action.

We must also not disrespect our ancestors and our relationship with nature and the Spirit world by allowing Western psychology to explain away what we are able to perceive with our intuitive minds.

Our intuitive minds allow us to call upon the emotional power required to actualize our creative potential and to; communicate with each other intuitively, i.e. being able to understand each other without an excessive use of words; and to be able to discern and foresee things outside of the perceived limitations of our sense organs.

SUGGESTIONS TO CULTIVATE INTUITION IN OUR CHILDREN:

1. **Inner Guidance** - Teach your child to ask, become quiet, and wait for inner guidance.

2. **Introspective Prayer** – Teach your child to pray the following manner: quiet the mind, surrender to Spirit, ask for guidance, and show gratitude.

3. **Meditation** - Meditation can amplify intuition. Teach your child to just "be still" and listen to his or her breathing. As a group many of us African Americans pray and ask, but never become still enough to hear God's answer.

4. **Dreams** - Intuition is said to be the language of dreams. Teach children to listen to their dreams. While dreams are symbolic, they are manifestations of our fears and good dreams are solutions to our problems.

5. **Contemplative Inspirational Reading and Oration** - Reading the Bible, Koran, Tanakh, and other Holy Books; and the recitation of verses from written Holy books and from oral Holy books such as the Ifa Corpus can provide guidance and direction to our children's lives. Other spiritual books and even biographies can be an inspiration to them as they travel the path to self-actualization.

6. **Physical Activities** - Certain movements open the natural energy channels located in the body. When open, one's intuitive mind is expanded to allow better interpretation of the information that it receives. Allow your child to participate in physical activities such as

African dance, African drumming, yoga, and capoeira.

9. CRITICAL THINKING

"The mere imparting of information is not education. Above all things, the effort must result in making a man think and do for himself."

Carter G. Woodson

A simple way to define critical thinking is the ability to cultivate one's own opinion on a subject as a result of contemplation using one's thinking and intuitive minds. It is analysis based on information received through the sense organs and reflected on through one's own connectedness to the situation, community, environment, world-at-large, and Spirit.

Our children are taught that their feelings and emotions are invalid and unworthy of acknowledgement. Also, they are taught that it is not proper to consider the perspective of a particular subject based on one's connection to a particular social or natural environment; they are supposed to be "objective"; therefore, by default, their point of view is aligned with the status quo, the interest of the majority culture, no matter whether this point of view benefits or detracts from their own reality.

There is no "objective"; it is impossible to extricate oneself from one's own life. The argument of "objectivity" is the means by which people are separated from critical contemplation and surrender their power and intellect to the status quo.

If there is to be any hope for our community, our children must have their critical intellectual abilities cultivated: they are our present and future.

CRITICAL THINKING AND POWER –

The Realization of Connections

At present our children simply see themselves as individually powerless cogwheels in a grand machine that promotes the idea of "creative scarcity" (only a few dreams can come true, and may require the sacrifice of others because of limited chances) which requires constant feeding through the consumption of material icons and the sacrificing of one's connections to others. The result of being processed by this machine is an "Individual", a person free of any and all 'connections'. This person is "free" of the "limitations" of culture, family, community, and nature. The grand irony being that one can only express one's personal power in the context of one's social relationships. So, if youth are allowed to condition themselves on the model that is taught to them through the media and increasingly through 'dis-connected' and irresponsible adults, they will develop an antagonistic attitude towards all others; because instead of being the framework of support on which one can build their life, others in the community, and even within the family, will be viewed as competition for limited resources. This growing trend of antagonism towards each other within the community is leading to a crisis in our relationships with each other – our families, our romantic relationships, our collective economics, our local communities, our greater community of African-descendant peoples, our relationships with nature, and our relationship with humanity as a whole.

Critical thinking is the realization of these connections in all that we do and all that we perceive.

OPPOSITION IDENTITY

Recent research says that our children are often disillusioned with school and develop an "opposition identity" because their experiences show them that getting an education does not pay off in the long run. They see people of color who have gotten an education being paid less and not getting the jobs that they deserve. The true purpose of education is not to get a job (that is however, what our schools program students to do). The purpose of education is to liberate a person to think critically. Literate and critical minded people are much less likely to be fooled by every new person and new idea that comes along. Talk to your child about the real purpose of becoming educated - learning to think for oneself.

THINK GLOBALLY

- Give your child "wings" as well as roots. Encourage him or her to think globally; to consider employment beyond U.S. borders. Our children need to develop an "immigrant" consciousness; if they cannot make it here, then go elsewhere to make their dreams come true. African Americans have a history of migration. We migrated North in the Great Migration. Exodusters went to Kansas and the Midwest. Other "free thinkers" went to Europe during the 1920's - 40's. Teach your child to not believe that the U.S. is the only place for them; the world belongs to them. Africans are all over the world.

LITERACY

- We must insist that all of our children learn to read. We must read with them. Every African home should have a library filled with African books.

FOREIGN LANGUAGES

- One of the most tangible ways that a child can learn about the differences between different worldviews and value systems in through the learning of other languages. Since language embodies the worldview of a culture, the learning of another language, essentially a non-Western language clearly illustrates to our children that many of the "truths", "realities", and perspectives of mainstream culture are culture-specific and not universal truths for all of the humanity.

PROPAGANDA VERSUS REALITY

Teach your children to read between the lines. At dinnertime, we should discuss current events. We should teach our how to discern propaganda and reality.

- Teach children how to read the newspaper.

- Teach children how to watch television.

- Teach children how to look at the news.

- Teach children how to use the Internet.

- Teach children that things (i.e. information) do not exist in and of themselves. Everything has a purpose. Hence, the information that they receive is to promote a particular purpose or agenda, whether positive or negative. Our children must be able to discern whether this information is designed to be for the interest or against their interests.

10. RITES OF PASSAGE/INITIATION

"The African has developed and organized a system useful to him for all the needs of life."

Edward Wilmot Blyden

ROLE DEFINITION

In the conquest of African peoples and in the destruction of African culture to convert Africans to a European worldview, an integral part of this strategy was in the destruction of Women's societies/Female Mysteries. Since it is by the sanction of the Mothers that the Male Mysteries are complete, eliminating the Female Mysteries ungrounds the Male Mysteries and leaves them incomplete. Without knowledge of these spiritual realities and adopting this new paternalistic worldview, men who are ignorant of our spirituality can be lead to believe that the existence of Male secret societies and organizations constitutes a rationale for male supremacy and misogyny, when, in truth, gendered secret societies exist to promote the spiritual potential inherent in both men and women. These societies rely on each other for grounding, spiritual balance, completion of initiations, and purpose of existence in contributing to the perpetuation of the family, community, and nation.

No matter what present-day manifestation that one can witness of collective male chauvinism in African or African-descendant societies, it can be said that, if so, this society has been radically affected by a non-African society which has a different spiritual worldview. In our cultures, from the standpoint of male spiritual or political leadership, the blessing and the sanction of the Mothers is required. There is no strong man without a strong woman somewhere in his life.

We must recreate this balance in the lives of our children. We are family. We do not have to have the same "battle of the sexes" that exists in the mainstream culture. Our sons and daughters only know what we teach them. If we teach them that one sex is of great value and can do no harm, while the other possesses half of the spiritual inheritance of the other and is derived from the lineage of the source of evil in the world, they will become this. Or even worse, if they are raised to view each other with suspicion and distrust, they will become this. We must raise our children to know their worth, and know that their worth does not depend of the diminishment or predication of those of the opposite sex. They must know that their sex does not diminish any potential aspirations for physical plane dreams, but enhances the spiritual potential for cultural roles that require particular male and female energy. We must teach our children that they exist to perform their inherent creative purposes on earth. There is no "superiority" in a balanced equation. We as men and women access the Source collectively $1 + 1 = 0$; or more correctly $0 + 1 =$ neutral/The Source. We as a community exist as a binary equation, born of our opposites, both having the latent traits and characteristics of our inverse. We cannot allow our children to grow up believing that some of us are of great value, while others are of diminished value. We are all valuable to each other, and we all suffer

166

if one of us does not have the opportunity to share their creativity with the community.

It is said that men have to dress like birds to travel in the world of Spirit. It is only from the Mothers than men can gain this power... All nature-based societies are essentially matriarchal, because in order for men to go to the world of Spirit, they must go dressed as birds, i.e. access female spirituality, either from cultivated female energy within themselves or given through the Mothers.

RITES OF PASSAGE

In the traditional African worldview, a system of socialization was established which focused on the moral and social development of youth. One of The most important stages of the boy or girl's life was the "rites of passage" which prepared them for manhood and womanhood. During this process the girl or boy learned the spiritual and cultural beliefs of their people and the purpose and responsibilities to the community. In African American communities the training of youth was initially carried out by families, called "home training" and reinforced in the community. With the crisis of values that our children now face, it is absolutely necessary that we restore a system of teaching traditional cultural values.

- *Initiate rights of passage programs*

  Our boys and girls need to be taught their cultural and community roles and responsibilities. Men and women's knowledge must be passed on the next generation. Information about being adult, body changes, parenthood, and spirituality needs to be taught to all of our children consistently.

- *Necessary discussions*

  Talk to your child about the roles and responsibilities of males and females. Talk about the respect that each must be given and why.

  Of course, talk to your child about sex and the role of procreation in the African worldview. Help them to understand the cultural dynamics of African marriages.

- ***Increase your knowledge***

  If you do not feel comfortable having the previously mentioned discussion, talk to an elder about how to proceed or read a book on the topic.

INITIATION

Initiation is the ritualized change from one period of life to next. We need to recreate initiation rituals and the "mysteries" (knowledges) that are shared with the initiate by the members of the period of life that they have entered into. For example, initiations can occur when a child enters school; when a child enters teenage years; when a teenager becomes a young women or man; at engagement and when couples are married; upon the birth of the first child; the naming of the child; when a woman reaches menopause; adoptions; reaching elderhood; and funerals.

RELATIONSHIPS

We have to teach our children the relationships are not for obtaining something from someone, but rather an opportunity to share wholly, and to be with someone whom you can comfortable to express 100% of who you are. We need to teach them that their mates enrich their lives. They do not "make them whole". They must be taught that they will not find "personal fulfillment" in the mate, they will find in within themselves through their personal efforts and achievements. What they will find in a mate is inspiration to achieve their creative potential and a lifelong life friend and lover to share life with. In our culture, a person's unconditional love needs are fulfilled through the family and community. There is no danger in losing oneself in romantic love relationships between the person is already whole, and they will not allow themselves to act in a way that violates this. We as adults have to reconstruct a community in which our children receive all of the love and encouragement that they need so that they can grow up to be whole, happy, emotionally healthy adults.

- **Modeling**

  Remember you teach your child more about how to treat the member of the opposite sex through your actions than your words. Model respect for yourself and respect for your partner.

11. POWER

*"There is a soul force in the universe,
which, if we permit it, will flow through
us and produce."*
Mohandas K. Gandhi

The experience of personal power is one of our basic human needs. Much of the crisis in values and the behavior that it generates in our children comes from their misguided attempts to achieve a sense of personal power in their lives. Mainstream culture promises a false power which comes through fame and fortune. Our children must understand that each culture serves the needs of its particular group; others who do not truly understand the workings and ins and outs of that culture become marginalized by its values. It is important for our children to understand "true" power. Before the enslavement and colonial periods Africans possessed true power; even among the enslaved, the majority lived with a sense of dignity and a sense of inner power that even the lash could not dislodge.

Our African-centered worldview teaches us that true power comes from our spiritual connection to God, our ancestors, and all within the universe. When our children are reconnected with their true culture, they will again experience personal power. There will be no need for them to search for it through the values of another culture.

SOURCES OF POWER

True power comes from three sources. There is being power which comes from our inner resources, our connection with Divine Mind; and our collective cultural mind. Our doing power comes from the "right" use of gifts and talents. Finally, our connecting power comes from our unity with others for a purpose and our collectivistic worldview. The negative power that our children see expressed in the world is power from domination; the controlling, oppressing, and exploiting of others. It is unfortunate that our children are learning this type of power from the lyrics of gangsta rap [5] and from popular video games.

---

[5] Repeated from Part I: There is a differentiation between hip-hop and gangsta rap. Those performing hip-hop understand and embrace the responsibility that comes with delivering the Spoken word, while

It is important for our children to understand the difference between abusive or false power and true power. Power in itself is very positive; it is only power from domination that causes problems in the world. We must teach our children about the dynamics of power and how to achieve a sense of personal power.

---

those performing "gangsta rap" have internalized a foreign value system based on individualistic materialism. Sadly there are some performers who are deemed "hip-hop artists" who actually fall into the category of "gangsta rap" because of their lack of consideration for our community.

BEING POWER

- **Spiritual Connection**

  The most important source of our being power is our spiritual connection. Besides and even more important than a particular religious connection, children need to be connected spiritually to the Creator, their ancestors, nature, and all the Universe.

- **Connecting Spiritually**

  As well as teaching our children to pray, we must also teach them how to "quiet the mind" or meditate so that they can hear the spiritual answers that are provided.

- *Visualization*

  One way to help our children tap their being power is to encourage their imagination. We must teach our children that if they can **see it, and believe it, they can achieve it.**

DOING POWER

- **"I Can"**

  The source of our children's doing power is their capabilities. The things that our children are able to accomplish give them a sense of power derived from "doing". Every child should be able to verbalize one thing that they can do well.

- **Gifts and Talents**

  Our role as adult guides to our children is to observe and to help them discover their unique and special gifts and talents. We must encourage and give them opportunities to develop these gifts and talents. You are not carrying out your responsibility if your child cannot

verbalize at least one gift or talent that

they have.

CONNECTING POWER

- *Collectivism*

  Our African-centered culture provides our children with a source of power. Through our oneness and connection to others we learn to know ourselves better, to express who we are, and to be of support to others. We are empowered by our identification with our group and working for the good of the group provides us with a deep sense of personal power.

OUR ROLE

One of the most important things that we can do to help our children overcome the crisis in values is to help them discover a sense of personal power. If they can understand what true power is, and how it they can tap it, they can then make the best of choices and live purposeful, fulfilling lives.

12. PURPOSE

"Man cannot live without some knowledge of the purpose of life. If he can find no purpose in life, he creates one in the inevitability of death."
Chester Himes

For African people, the expression of one's life purpose and the alignment between one's two heads, the mind and the heart are the most important things. African society and spirituality are based on the expression of creative purpose.

During slavery we had the total opposite experience. We were turned into property and had no control over our lives. One could not even have a family – one's wife, husband, or children could be sold away at any time and you would never see them again. We had to live to serve someone else's purpose. This was the antithesis of being an African.

In the post-slavery times up until Integration, education was a revolutionary act; one in which we fought for the freedom to actualize ourselves. In the post-Integration times, we sacrificed our children for the idea that instant gratification and consumption is easier than the slower but more fulfilling process of cultivating creative potential. It is easier just to do what it takes to get a "good" job that does not utilize one's creative potential (rather than a job that does utilize one's creative potential or creating a business that does), or some other fast means of income production so that you could buy the material icons needed to measure one's worse through the comparison of possessions with others.

LIFE PURPOSE

Our purpose in life is to use our unique gifts and talents in the service of our people. In African cultures, the most important component of child's intellectual and spiritual life is in the discovery of his or her passion, or dreams. It is from knowledge of this that the adults in the community design the child's educational offerings to fit the cultivation of this young mind and offer support, advice, and encouragement in this field of study so that he or she con contribute their creative gifts to the community and enrich the lives of all.

We can witness the lack of purpose in our youth through their lack of imagination and creativity: In the past, kids would create their own fashions, now they buy brands and take on "identities" as "brand consumers". Individual style

187

was once celebrated; emulating others is now fashion – all the young men who wear sports paraphernalia as clothes with other people's names on their backs - devoid of their own identities. Our children used to dream a variety of dreams – scientists, astronauts, healers, bankers, doctors, builders, nurses, teachers, professors, presidents, drummers, dancers, singers, Olympic medalists, "making that paper" is all that matters, and the usual route of perceived success in this endeavor is through being a professional sport player (basketball or football) and through rapping.

Nothing is wrong with our youth desiring to be professional sportsmen or rappers, but what is missing in this equation is 1) contemplation over whether this is one's actual reason for existing on this planet, 2) whether one is willing to work hard enough to turn their sports playing or lyrical delivery into an art form.

African culture in the US has been extremely marginalized in the past decade. The "marginal" that I mean does not "pushed to the side", but instead "of mediocre quality". The quest to create art solely for commerce has lead to the destruction of the integrity of our art forms; and we have given away the power to criticize our art forms for their prowess and suitability to our culture, to the mainstream. Lyrics over the last 10 years have largely been devoid of any political consciousness or responsibility to the community.

We must raise the bar on the culture that we produce. Not just anybody can be authorized to use the "word power" on our people. It is our tradition that our storytellers support the community through the sharing of verse, not cannibalizing it through the sharing of verse.

This trend is indicative of an even greater phenomenon - the absence of imagination in our children. Our children no longer dream. Our children's "dreams" are those of adults who have given up on their dreams and are looking for the quickest scheme that can make them some money to get them out of a financial hardship, temporarily.

We have allowed our children to receive their dreams from television shows, music videos, video games, Internet sites, and the radio. Children are not adults. Adults can be exposed to a variety of media and maintain the integrity of who they are. Children are at a very formative stage in which they are sponges who learn and emulate what they are taught by those older than them. If they are not engaged with the discourse of "who are you?" and "what do you see yourself doing in 20 years", the video screen will answer this question for them. As the African proverb says "Children not taught by their parents will be taught by the world".

The reason that our children exist is to actualize their created purpose. They came to this Earth to share something special of the Creator. If we do not take our responsibility as adults, which is to cultivate the latent creative potential of our children, we will be essentially killing them, because they exist to be purposeful. A purposeless person is only taking up space until they die.

When we avoid our responsibility in cultivating every young mind, we are telling the Creator that we do not want any solutions to our problems and that we desire not to exist.

Teaching purpose is our job; and it is the source of our greatest joy. There is nothing more beautiful that witnessing someone actualizing their purpose. They become living art. In traditional African culture, the role that the community plays is the supportive network in which everyone is aware of everyone else's purpose, so each person assists each other in improving his or her art; hence the community benefits from the contribution of each person. And all adults are made aware of each child's passion and dreams so that their education and opportunities are geared to actualizing this purpose as adults in the community.

HOW TO TEACH ABOUT PURPOSE:

1. **Do What You Love** – Perhaps better than encouraging your child to get an education to make a lot of money, encourage her to "do what she loves and the money will come". When we are using our gifts and talents in service, we usually love what we do. Work does not seem like work; we are fully one with our work and our purpose when this occurs.

2. Practice the 4As[5]

The 4 A's[6] that can be used to increase one's personal power to actualize their Life Purpose. Teach your children to:

Acknowledge their personal assets (one's strengths, gifts, talents, skills, and abilities). We all have them. They just have to do the work of identifying theirs. You are to help them look within and discover their strengths, gifts, talents, skills, and abilities.

Accept their personal assets. Now that they have found these assets, they must own them. They must believe that they are worthy to possess these assets. It is sometimes

---

[5] From Bireda, Martha R. Ph.D. (2007) *Pathway to Change: A Guide to Personal Empowerment*. Tokyo: blue ocean press.
[6] Ibid.

difficult for us to accept all of the good things about ourselves.

Affirm their personal assets. Tell them to say them out loud. Remind them daily of all the good things that they have going for them.

Act upon their personal assets. Teach them to use their strengths, gifts, talents, skills, and abilities to create the life that they desire.

3. Recognizing Being, Doing, Connecting, Power[7]

Being Power

We cannot know our purpose without understanding our spiritual nature and connecting with God, Allah, Jehovah, Infinite Mystery, Olorun, Spirit, The Creator, the Source, the Supreme Being, or called by whatever name one chooses.

Doing Power

An affirmation (or statement of truth) that we should teach our children to say: "I offer my skills, gifts, talents in the service of God." When they recognize the spiritual nature of

---

[7] Ibid.

their capabilities, they will easily be able to connect with their purpose.

Connecting Power

If our children are on the path to actualizing their Purpose, then it is important that their friends be on similar paths. It is our responsibility as parents to know the character of our children's friends and the character of their parents. I can remember that anytime a new playmate showed up in my life, my grandmother would ask, "Honey, who is your momma?" It was the "character" not the wealth or position of the adults in that child's life that was important. My grandmother ensured that my connecting power would keep me in line with my purpose.

4. Teach your children three keys to empowerment (actualizing their purpose) PCD[8]: Purpose, Direction, Commitment.

Teach your children three keys to empowerment **PCD**[9]: Purpose, Direction, Commitment.

Purpose: Our destiny as human beings is to fully actualize or reach our highest potential. Our **purpose** is to manifest the destiny for which we were created by using our unique gifts and talents in service to our community and society.

Direction: Our **direction** determines their life course or path. It is the steps that we take to achieve or live own life purpose. We are familiar and comfortable with the present

---

[8] Ibid.
[9] Ibid.

life pattern, so when we choose a new life course or path, we must decide the steps or direction we will take.

Commitment: Our **commitment** is our dedication to our new life path and achieving or living our purpose. It determines our ability to "stay the course", and to "hang on" when things get tough. Life is not always easy, but if we connect to the Higher Power, tap into our inner resources, and use our personal assets we will find that we have the personal power necessary to achieve despite the odds.

5. Create a Life Road Map[10]

Under NO CIRCUMSTANCES do you allow your child to put any limitations on their dreams, i.e. money, location, connections, etc. Dreams have no limitations. If one's dreams are translated into one's life purpose, they will find the way, despite any apparent present-day obstacles to actualizing this purpose and their dreams. Every successful person saw themselves doing and being who they are long before this became a physical plane reality. This is because, once they saw their purpose clearly, they made all of the choices and allotted the necessary time to skill development to make that "visible" dream a reality.

---

[10] Ibid.

A Life Road Map consists of the following:

- Life purpose

- Life goals

- Beliefs they hold about themselves and their life

- Ways in which they will tap your being, doing, and connecting power

- Inner resources

- Personal assets

- Skills they will learn and practice

- The outcome they expect (i.e. 5, 10, 15 years from now)

These processes should be started as early as possible in a child's life. It is never too late to cultivate purpose, for it is our reason for existing. But, it is easier to convince a child of the viability of their dreams the less discouraging messages that they have received. The more that they have received, the harder that we have to work to not allow them to believe these things and to visualize themselves being and doing who their truly are.

PART IV.

THE CHILD RETURNS HOME

If we equip our children with the twelve traditional values discussed in this book, they can survive racism, oppression, and exploitation. They will be able to successfully negotiate their place in the global world of the 21st century. Attachment to culture provides a foundation and an identity that cannot easily be dislodged. Attachment to culture gives a sense of belonging, builds character, fortifies our strength, and enables us to go within to tap our greatest resources. With our guidance and with a set of beliefs, values, and norms that have enabled generations of Africans to survive and to thrive, our children will have the ability to live in mainstream but not be of it. Rather than the consciousness of a caste minority that produces the need to be approved, accepted, and assimilate into the mainstream, our children will adopt a consciousness that cannot be infiltrated by destructive values. Africans in America have survived and lived with dignity despite enslavement, racial oppression, and economic exploitation. If we adults step forward and accept the responsibility given to us by the Creator and our ancestors, our children will stand tall in the face of a culture that threatens their very existence and emerge victorious.

CHILDREN AND YOUTH

Children and youth are the main focus of indoctrination by the perpetuators of the mainstream culture. Children and youth are targeted because of their vulnerability and pivotal role in transmitting the mainstream to future generations. They are indoctrinated through four means: the mass media; the Internet; the behavior of parents; and the school system, if the targeted society becomes dominated to the extent that they are no longer in control of what is taught in the schools.

1. Children and youth must be involved in the educational process through a Character Education Program that emphasizes the three pillars of a humanitarian and civil

society: Purpose, Connectedness, and Service.

2. The Character Education Program must be implemented at the primary and secondary levels as part of the standard school curriculum.

PARENTS/FAMILIES

Parents/families are the most socializing agents of the mainstream culture. When parents embrace the values of the mainstream culture, children will imitate them. If parents and family members focus on making money and accumulating things, children will become participants in the same process.

Parents must:

1. Evaluate their behavior and ask, "What are we teaching our children?"
2. Model behavior that teaches purpose, connectedness, and service.
3. Change behaviors if focusing on accumulation of money or things.

4. Encourage intrinsic motivation/gratification in children.

5. Limit exposure to the mainstream culture through television and the Internet. They will have their entire adult lives to choose what they want to watch and listen to. You have form the foundation of their value system and critical thinking systems so that they can consume media proactively, not passively.

6. Talk to children about the purpose of television ads and shows.

7. Talk to children about the unrealistic lifestyles portrayed on television.

8. Talk to children about "real life" in the mainstream culture.

9. Talk to children about the dangers of individualism, selfishness, greed, and materialism.

10. Talk to children about the positive aspects of their cultural beliefs, values, and norms.

11. Do not succumb to children's desires to have products from the mainstream culture, i.e. branded clothes and other items. Discuss needs vs. wants.

12. Join with other parents/families to find ways to reject the undesirable aspects of mainstream culture and embrace our traditional culture and worldview.

COMMUNITY

It is through the transformation of the belief system of the targeted group that the mainstream culture takes hold in a society. Community solidarity and cultural integrity are the means by which the targeted society can prevent being overtaken and dominated by the mainstream culture. The community must:

1. Join forces to reject the undesirable values of the mainstream culture.

2. Come together to affirm the beliefs, values, and norms of the traditional culture.

3. Reinforce the values of purpose, connectedness, and service.

4. Ostracize individualism, selfishness, greed, materialism and other behaviors of the

mainstream culture that do not promote the welfare of the group.

The influence of African American youth is felt worldwide; they have become "conveyers of culture". In Singapore, youth dress like them; in Tokyo they imitate their music and hairstyles, on the Micronesian island of Yap, young Yapese males are referred to as "Black American wannabes" because of their imitation of the dress and mannerism of African Americans. But in places like Britain, West Indian parents complain that their youth are emulating the negative aspects of the behavior of African American youth, and these complaints will grow, expanding outside of the Diaspora and throughout other parts of the world.

People worldwide have looked to African Americans as an example of a determined people with a strong sense of cultural integrity, and are still celebrated our resistance of colonialism throughout the Diaspora and for the Civil Rights struggle in the US. In the larger picture, we still do represent the face of self-determination, success in the struggle for social justice, spirituality, success in spite of tremendous adversity, and of innovation and creativity, but if we continue to allow our youth to embody the Culture of Conspicuous Consumption and Individualistic Materialism and to act as its ambassadors, our high level of respect, admiration, and cultural influence in the world will diminish.

If our children come to know their true selves and reconnect with their true culture, just imagine the tremendously powerful and positive

214

influence that African American youth can have on young people across the world. African American children are very special and they can be not only a gift to us, but a gift to the world. It is our duty to ensure that they carry out their purpose and role.

Bibliography

Bireda, Martha R. (2002) *Eliminating Racial Profiling in School Discipline: Cultures in Conflict*. Alexandria: Scarecrow Press.

Bireda, Martha R. (2007) *Pathway to Change: A Guide to Emotional Transformation*. Tokyo: blue ocean press.

Bireda, Martha R. (2007) *The Trabue Woods Book of Values*. Tokyo: blue ocean press.

Bireda, Martha R. & Cummings, Jaha F. (2008) *Preserving Cultural Integrity in the Age of Globalization*. Tokyo: blue ocean press.

Cummings, J.F. (2008) *How to Rule to World: Lessons in Conquest for the Modern Prince*. Tokyo: blue ocean press.

Fatunmbi, Falokun Awo (2006) *Family Spirit: The Ifa' Concept of Egun*. Brooklyn, NY: Athelia Henrietta Press.

Fleming, Robert (1996). The Wisdom of the Elders. NY: Ballentine Books.

long, p.w. (2006) *Cuba is State of Mind: The Spiritual Traveler, Vol. I*. Tokyo: blue ocean press

Newman, Richard (2000). *African American Quotations*. New York: Checkmark Books.

Some', Sobonfu E. (1999). *Welcome Spirit Home: Ancient African Teachings To Celebrate Children and Community*. Novato, CA: New World Library

OMOWALI VILLAGE RETREATS

The Child Returns Home

Reconnecting Our Children With Their True Culture

Weekend Intergenerational Retreats
Sponsored By Your Church or
Organization

For Information Contact:
Martha R. Bireda, Ph.D.
(941)639-2914 or (239)823-2911
biredagrp@aol.com

Aoishima Research Institute presents

The Character Education and Cultural Preservation Book Development Project

- We offer a curriculum development program that enables entities to develop character/values education and cultural preservation programs.
- We assist clients from Consultation through the Publishing of the materials.
- At the end of the process clients will have published texts that can be used for their character/values education and cultural preservation needs.

The following is an excerpt explaining to children the importance of values. This excerpt is from the book, *The Trabue Woods Book on Values*:

"WHY WE SHOULD LEARN ABOUT VALUES"

Values are what a group of people feel are important. Our values help us to decide what is right or wrong. They guide our actions. They are like signs on the highway, they point out the right direction in which we are to go. Our values help to determine our character. When we say that a person has good character, we are talking about their values. This book is about values. One way in which we can learn about values is to study history and learn about the values of historical figures. In this book, we will learn about the values of a group of African American pioneers who settled in southwest Florida in 1885, and helped to establish the town of Trabue, later called Punta Gorda, on the Charlotte Harbor. While these African Americans lived in many parts of what became known as Charlotte County, they established their own special community named Trabue Woods."

For more information please contact:

Martha R. Bireda, Ph.D.

The Bireda Group, P.O. Box 510818, Punta Gorda, Florida 33951
Telefax: (941) 639-2914
E-mail: biredagrp@aol.com or mail@aoishima-research.com

AOISHIMA RESEARCH INSTITUTE
CULTURAL PRESERVATION WORKSHOP SERIES
Traditional African American Values

1. **Omowali: The Child Returns Home**

   Focuses on how traditional values and cultural integrity can be restored in African American communities.

2. **Reclaiming The Cultural Self**

   Learning how to overcome attachment to cultural values other than one's own (cultural alienation) and to reconstruct belief and value systems that promote a culturally-affirmed life.

3. **Cultural Legacy: Values That Support and Sustain**

   An examination of the values that helped African Americans (1885 -1925) to survive and build thriving communities while living through one of the most difficult periods African Americans faced, with the exception of slavery. Focuses on the pioneers of the Trabue Woods community in Punta Gorda, Florida.

4. **Lessons From The Ancestors**

   Addresses how the beliefs and values of the ancestors can be applied to solve problems and live more fully in the 21st century.

5. **Community History That Every African American Child Should Know**

   Strategies to help African American youth learn the essentials of their local history.

6. **The Essentials of Developing A Cultural Repository**

   Strategies for helping community organizations collect, preserve, and educate regarding local history.

For more information please contact:

Martha R. Bireda, Ph.D.
The Bireda Group,
P.O. Box 510818
Punta Gorda, Florida 33951

Telefax: (941) 639-2914
E-mail: biredagrp@aol.com
Website: http://biredagroup.com

Other Selected Titles by blue ocean press

The Trabue Woods Book of Values
By Martha R. Bireda, Ph.D.
(2007)
ISBN: 978-4-902837-20-X

The traditional values held by the pioneers that settled the Trabue Woods Community enabled the community to survive and to thrive. These values passed generation to generation fro 1885 to the late 1960's were learned by the author herself as a girl growing up in the Trabue Woods community. Using old photographs and newspaper articles, the 8 core values learned by the children of Trabue Woods are shared with young readers ages 8 – 12. The values taught in Trabue woods are typical of those held by the descendents of slaves who established communities after the turn of the century.

Pathway to Change:
A Guide to Personal Transformation
by Martha R. Bireda, Ph.D. (2007)
ISBN: 978-4-902837-47-1

Pathway To Change is a holistic approach to personal transformation that is based upon cognitive behavioral theory and emphasizes cognitive restructuring or belief system change. Participants in the process learn how to identify and modify erroneous and self-defeating beliefs and values that have led to poor choices and negative behaviors in the past. Correctional interventions that include a cognitive skills component have been found to have strong research support for their effectiveness.

Pathway to Change is a cognitive restructuring program that was created to break of cycle of self-destructive thoughts and behaviors in incarcerated populations. It has been implemented in prisons in the US for 10 years and has been highly effectively in reducing the recidivism rates for the inmates who have gone through this process. Ideally participants are taken through Pathway to Change process by a certified PTC facilitator, but over the years we have found that this process is also effective on persons that seriously engage in the process of groups of their own making. This book is both a workbook for participants in a facilitated PTC workshop, as well as a tool for individual personal transformation for anyone who is "stuck".

In addition to its uses for self-therapy and anti-recidivism programs, PTC can also used as very effective tool in Workforce Development, Youth, Personal Empowerment, Employee Placement and Development, Career Counseling, Domestic Violence (for both perpetrators and victims), Substance Abuse, Delinquency Prevention, and Microenterprise/ Entrepreneurship Programs.

**Parables of Milk and Might: Development Political Satire -
»The Voices of the Affected«**
by RAN (2008)
ISBN: 978-4-902837-21-8

Following over four decades of development politics, after the official end of colonialism in most countries in Africa, South America and Asia, it is difficult for the industrial countries to forgo their economic interests in the developing countries, which are said to be independent. Their continued presence in these countries, controlling, or dictating the trend of economic and political developments, is a proof of the protection of their interests.

Parables of Milk and Might is a satire on the international development sector, in particular, the relationship between the countries of the Global North and South. The book uses a wonderful combination of wordplay, metaphor, and humorous storytelling to get its message across. It has the feel of *Animal Farm*, but instead of animals, uses human beings with colorful personalities.

From the author:

The main purpose for writing this book is to use it to sensitize many people, both in the industrial countries, as well as in the developing world, particularly in Africa and in Asia, the Caribbean and South American countries, about the negative effects of the global economic system, which is controlled by the powerful and wealthy countries, to the disadvantage of the developing countries. This sensitization will increase the awareness of people about the effects of this negative development, which is the cause of poverty, underdevelopment and conflicts in the world."

This book is translated from its original German.

(Written by a Ghanaian author who resides in Germany)

How To Rule the World:
Lessons in Conquest by the Modern Prince
by J.F. Cummings (2008)
ISBN: 978-4-902837-00-5

How to Rule the World provides a satirical commentary on today's "modern world" and the "forces" that govern it. This is done in the voice of "civilization's" greatest supporter, an advisor to the Prince. How to Rule the World is a modern adaptation of Machiavelli's The Prince.

The author provides the reader, the Prince, with a methodology of non-invasive influence and control that will grant them sovereignty over their desired target nation-state and eventually over the world-at-large.

How to Rule the World shows the modern Prince how to utilize "modern ideals" such as free trade, democratic governance, human rights, freedom and individual rights, rule of law, and free press to exert control over other nations and convince them to collaborate in their own domination and exploitation through their quest to do whatever is required of them to be accepted as "developed", "modern" nations. Though adherence to the methodology of conquest explained in the book, the Prince will be granted access to the psyche of the target nation's population and will be able to redefine its very sense of worth and self-definition.

How to Rule the World, is written in first-person like Machiavelli's, The Prince, and is a conversation with the reader, leading to self-examination his or her own value system, thought processes, and concepts of human nature. It provides a forum through which the reader can determine his or her position in the world and within their own psyche as 'Prince' or 'subject', and how the actions of both impact on the very sustainability of the human species.

From the 1898 Consciousness Studies Series by

blue ocean press

Cuba is a State of Mind
(The Spiritual Traveler, Vol. I)
By p.w. long
(2006)
ISBN: 978-4-902837-18-8

From the Spiritual Traveler Series, a group of travelers reveal truths about Cuba yet realized by most readers. This is a wonderful journey into the living consciousness that is called "Cuba", and the stories of those who live there.

"A Tourist takes in the local sights;
a Traveler sees the reality of a landscape."

About the Authors

Martha R. Bireda, Ph.D.:

Dr. Bireda has been committed to teaching traditional African-American values and the empowerment of African-American children. She is the author of the Trabue Woods of Book of Values, a book for young readers ages 8-12. This book describes the values taught in the Trabue Woods community which are typical of those held by the descendants of slaves who established communities after the turn of the century. Dr. Bireda is also the Founder of the Blanchard House – Museum of African-American History and Culture. She is also the author of several books and co-author with Mr. Cummings of *Preserving Cultural Integrity in the Age of Globalization (2nd Edition is being released in late 2008)*. She is an Ikofa and Akpetebi in the Cuban/Lucumi tradition.

Jaha F. Cummings:

Mr. Cummings is an active researcher and the publisher of a Tokyo-based think tank. His professional and personal work deals with the following subjects: Education, Media, and Values Formation; Culture-based National Development Planning; The Significance of Cultural Center; Black Consciousness throughout the African Diaspora; and Methods of Cultivating the Creative Potential of Individuals. He has over 15 years experience in implementing youth, economic, organizational, governmental, and community development projects in both the public and private sectors internationally. He is the author of two other books and is the co-author with Dr. Bireda of *Preserving Cultural Integrity in the Age of Globalization (2nd Edition is being released in late 2008)*. He is an Awo Ifa (Babalawo) in the Cuban/Lucumi tradition.

Ordering blue ocean press books:

Individual Orders:

Books can be purchased and ordered from your local bookstore.

Books can also be purchased online through retailers such as: the Amazon.com family (amazon.com, amazon.co.jp, amazon.co.uk, amazon.fr, amazon.ca, amazon.de), Barnes and Nobles (bn.com, barnesandnobles.com), Powells.com, Abebooks.com, Alibris.com, etc.

Institutional Buyers, Booksellers, and Libraries:

Books can be ordered from the following distributors and wholesalers:

U.S. and Canada:
Ingram Book Group (ipage/Ingram, Ingram Library Services, Ingram International)
Baker & Taylor
NASCORP (a wholly-owned, for-profit subsidiary of the National Association of College Stores)

U.K. and Rest of World:
Gardners Books
Bertrams
Baker & Taylor
Ingram International